D0005796

Tracy

Seasons of Sharing

A Kasen Renku Collaboration

Thanks for sharing
your poetry and your
caring self with Indiana

Joyce Brinkman
Nov. 29, 2018

Seasons of Sharing

A KASEN RENKU COLLABORATION

Joyce Brinkman & Carolyn Kreiter-Foronda

with Catherine Aubelle, Flor Aguilera García, Gabriele Glang, & Kae Morii

Leapfrog Press
Fredonia, New York

Seasons of Sharing: A Kasen Renku Collaboration © 2014
by Joyce Brinkman and Carolyn Kreiter-Foronda,
with Catherine Aubelle, Flor Aguilera García, Gabriele Glang,
and Kae Morii

All rights reserved under International and
Pan-American Copyright Conventions

No part of this book may be reproduced, stored in a data base or other
retrieval system, or transmitted in any form, by any means, including
mechanical, electronic, photocopy, recording or otherwise, without the
prior written permission of the publisher.

Published in 2014 in the United States by
Leapfrog Press LLC
PO Box 505
Fredonia, NY 14063
www.leapfrogpress.com

Printed in the United States of America

Distributed in the United States by
Consortium Book Sales and Distribution
St. Paul, Minnesota 55114
www.cbsd.com

First Edition

ISBN: 978-1-935248-63-7

Library of Congress Cataloging-in-Publication Data

Available from the Library of Congress

Acknowledgments

The poem "Autumn Rain" first appeared in the following publication:

Tipton Poetry Journal (Issue #19, Fall 2010)

We have included a translation in the home language of each of our partners. We thank Gabriele Glang, Catherine Aubelle, Flor Aguilera García, and Kae Morii for this extra effort. While Carolyn and I have some familiarity with Spanish, French, and German, we could not have accomplished the quality translations produced by our European and North American friends. We were totally reliant on our friend Kae for any use of Japanese, and thank her, not only for that effort, but for her total commitment to poetry and global harmony.

Preface

In 2007, it was my pleasure to host the 3rd Biennial Gathering of Poets Laureate in Indiana. Besides US state poets laureate we were also fortunate to have two international poets at the Gathering. Both of our international poets had written haiku and one, Kae Morii of Japan, celebrated it as part of her cultural heritage. Knowing that Japan is a more structured society than the US, I had worried whether American poets would provide too much culture shock for our Japanese guest, but Kae's delightful personality and her deep respect for all cultures proved infectious. Her presence caused me to begin reading and then writing Asian forms of poetry.

My interest spilled over to another state laureate, Carolyn Kreiter-Foronda of Virginia. We asked Kae, now back in Japan, if she would join us in writing a kasen renku. We wanted to use the traditional English 5–7–5 syllable count and some of the traditional images — moon, flower, love — but we wanted to abandon the traditional seasonal movements to concentrate our renku on just one season. Carolyn and I are avid lovers of wildlife, and the Asian focus on nature certainly appealed to us. We wanted our renku to reflect the natural environment from three different global points and to weave into the poem human events from those locations and from the broader world during one season of the year.

Kae Morii proved a superb partner for our Autumn renku. Writing renku by e-mail with this skilled poet became as infectious as her personality. Opening an e-mail to find the latest verse was a much anticipated event, and we quickly moved through the 36 verses hungry for more. Kae's participation had added to the authenticity of our work, and her global perspective provided inspiration to expand our activities to include even more cultures.

We kept our single-season focus as Carolyn and I proceeded to Winter, Spring, and Summer renku with bilingual poets from Germany (Gabriele Glang), France (Catherine Aubelle), and Mexico (Flor Aguilera García). Kae had automatically translated our Autumn poem into Japanese, and each subsequent poet also translated her work into her home country's language.

As a poet and program chair for a small poetry not-for-profit, I have promoted and participated in many artistic collaborations. In America, I think we suffer from what I call the Dickinson/Thoreau syndrome. Too often we view the poet as a recluse alone with personal thoughts and words. For early Japanese renga poets, poetry was a wonderful word party. Today, thanks to the internet, that party can span the globe. It is one world, and the renga relationships I enjoy enable me to connect with other poets and see the natural world from their place on our planet.

I began each renku with a three line 5–7–5 syllable verse, and one of our global partners responded with a two line 7–7 syllable verse. Carolyn Kreiter-Foronda wrote each trailing 5–7–5 syllable verse, which is followed by another 7–7 syllable verse from the global partner. This pattern is followed on each page of the book. It is important to remember that a renku is not a narrative in the sense of having a plot. For our mono-thematic renku, the only story derives from the season during which each renku was written. Each verse plays off the preceding verse, while reflecting the poem's season from a different geographic location. Renku verses are connected, but they also can stand alone, which is why the haiku developed from them.

Doing these kasen renku has been one of life's most enjoyable poetry experiences. Writing renku expands your knowledge of poetry and the world. It's reward-ing to share through carefully crafted words what you are experiencing during a specific time of the year and equally edifying to be surprised and delighted with the words collaborators share in return. Creating with our global friends could have been better only if there were more seasons in a year. Writing these kasen renku has truly produced rich Seasons of Sharing.

Joyce Brinkman
Indiana Poet Laureate 2002–2008
Kasen Renku Sabaki

Contents

Spring Light

Joyce Brinkman, Catherine Aubelle, Carolyn Kreiter-Foronda

Leap night's moon lingers.
One small sliver left to shine
before a French spring.

A thin slit in dawn's membrane
slakes remote lines' thirst with yolk.

Pileated wood-
peckers drum dead oaks. Sexy
males alert for mates.

Staccato telegraphers . . .
though first blooms discuss at length.

Jade Rabbit pounds herbs.
Black rice cakes form in darkness.
Listen to the moon!

The cinnamon tree sways us
as it breathes ambrosial tales.

Lucent butterfly.
Stir midday sun like a balm —
fragrant, curative.

Sheer glints scrawled on gibbous waves:
love's stream moored to golden carp . . .

Solar seduction.
Venus, Jupiter unite,
trails of solitude.

Striding lost lands for such trysts,
one curlew cries — Loplop soars!

Red-winged blackbirds wake,
dazzle the wild dogwood's blush —
morning's companions.

Sanguine illuminations
on sheets of sky dyed with woad.

Persian lilac smells
embrace the peony moon.
Pink snow paths perish.

Blood beats in Baroque paeans —
Heed the walking bass and dance!

Steamy mist shimmies
blue jacaranda leaves — sweet
sensual salsa.

The diurnal star proffers
its flesh to swags of shadows.

Happy Valley floor
shaded by wisteria —
seeds of stellar growth.

. . . Thrown at random. Nude pages —
fallows in the pergola.

Tail cocked, plucky wren
serenades chicks, tucked in eaves.
A soulful sol-fa.

De dicto, Ishtar recalls
her swains' names. Souls dehisce.

Bindweed lays herself
bare. Go forth to multiply!
Latent brides of white.

Longing necklaces . . . for a bead
of alabaster, each year.

Pearl strands fall. Laurel
blossoms paint the florid earth.
Whispers of ivory.

Weighty hints of tenderness,
dotted notes on time's keyboard . . .

Evening harmony . . .
quiet rifts, disjunctive yeowls.
Calico cat flirts.

Hours intertwine with seconds
purring in arabesque scrolls.

Damselflies, smitten,
flutter in midair — orbed eyes
twinkling, hearts on fire.

Snoozing in the heat. Flashes
coruscate beneath lashes.

Ordinary moon —
not your point of perigee.
Devotee stays close.

Two nightingales dialogue;
gems ricochet in the dusk.

Down from hickories
screech owls dive, shrill calls soaring —
woodland ecstasy.

Our summer dresses! There, in
half opened poppies' gussets!

Purple coneflowers
await solstice. Survivors!
Surmount dry seasons.

Cerulean canopy. . . .
Someone in the Other's husk.

Hummingbirds sip wine
from crimson trumpets, blaring.
Sunrise tantara.

A bound athwart the Big Pond
and intercalated days.

Lumière de printemps
(Spring Light)

Translated by Catherine Aubelle

Un jour sauté, la lune traîne.
Une petite mèche laissée pour briller
devant un printemps français.

Une fine entaille dans la membrane de l'aube
comble la soif des lignes éloignées, avec du jaune.

Le grand pic tambourine
sur les vieux chênes. L'alerte sélective
des mâles pour les copains.

Télégraphes en staccato . . .
Mais les premières éclosions discutent à plein.

Le lapin de Jade pile des herbes.
Des galettes de riz noir se forment dans l'obscurité.
Ecoute la lune !

Sous l'emprise de l'arbre à cannelle
qui nous souffle des contes ambrosiaques.

Papillons luisants.
Remuer le soleil de midi comme un baume —
odorant, curatif.

Des lueurs saillantes griffonnées sur les vagues gibbeuses :
le flot de l'amour ancré aux carpes dorées . . .

Séduction solaire.
Vénus, Jupiter s'unissent,
sentiers de solitude.

Sillonnant les terres perdues pour de telles entrevues,
un courlis crie — Loplop s'élève !

Des carouges à épaulettes remuent,
éblouissent le rouge du cornouiller —
compagnons du matin.

Illuminations sanguines
sur des feuilles de ciel teintées au pastel.

Les senteurs du lilas perse
étreignent les pivoines —
des chemins de neige rose périssent.

Le sang bat dans les chants baroques —
entends la marche de la basse et danse !

Une brume vaporeuse frémit
des feuilles du jacaranda bleu — douce,
sensuelle salsa.

L'étoile diurne profère
sa chair aux festons d'ombres.

Le sol de Happy Valley
ombragé par la glycine —
des pousses de graines stellaires.

. . . Jetées au hasard. Pages nues —
friches dans la pergola.

La queue dressée, le vaillant roitelet
donne la sérénade aux femelles, nichées dans les combles.
Un sol-fa sentimental.

De dicto, Ishtar se souvient
du nom de ses amants. Les âmes s'ouvrent.

Le liseron s'étale à nu.
Allez, multipliez-vous !
Latentes épouses de blanc.

Des colliers espérant . . . Une perle
d'albâtre, chaque année.

Des oboles tombent. Les fleurs
de lauriers peignent la terre ornée.
Murmures d'ivoire.

Nuances graves de tendresse,
notes pointées sur le clavier du temps . . .

Harmonie du soir . . .
Disputes paisibles, miaous disjonctifs.
Calico le chat flirte.

Les heures s'entrelacent avec les secondes,
ronronnent en volutes d'arabesques.

Les libellules, radieuses,
virevoltent en plein ciel — les yeux mi-clos
clignant, le cœur en feu.

Somnolence dans la chaleur. Des éclats
brillent sous les cils.

Lune ordinaire —
pas ton point de périgée.
Le dévot reste proche.

Deux rossignols dialoguent ;
ricochet de joyaux dans le crépuscule.

Dessous les caryers
les chats huants plongent, appels stridents s'élevant —
extase des bois.

Nos robes d'été ! Là, dans les
goussets de pavots semi-ouverts !

Des centaurées mauves
attendent le solstice. Rescapées !
Surmontez la saison sèche.

Canopée d'azur . . .
Quelqu'un dans l'écale de l'Autre.

Les colibris sirotent le vin
des trompettes incarnates, hurlantes.
Chant du lever de soleil.

Un bond à travers le Big Pond
et les jours intercalaires.

Summer Wind

Joyce Brinkman, Flor Aguilera García, Carolyn Kreiter-Foronda

Summer wind blows south,
pours heat on expectant night.
Moon melts into dawn.

Days swim up rivers like carp
slowly into dusky seas.

Skies flare and flicker.
Lightning bugs pierce ebony
screens of mist aglow.

Happy tears from Tlaloc's reign
welcoming the tender corn.

Clouds shroud the Mead Moon.
Here prayers come from flat ground.
Fathers cry — dogs search.

Tanagers nestled above
plead mercy from Feathered Snake.

Abandoned Deadrise,
upturned by a tornado,
where are your ghosts now?

They've become Zephyr and Breeze —
sweet tropical caresses.

Two geese with goslings.
Strong family affections
grow to mount Eurus.

Black meadows of swaying silk.
Waves in a lunar slow dance.

Stars ethereal
settle on wheat stacks gleaming:
a prism of gems.

Dawn's bird songs: tweet and twiddle,
fall silent when morning rains.

Shards of moonlight plunge
through ash — patterns cut on green.
White lilies quiver.

Hummingbirds feast, sad nectars.
Agave blues are in bloom.

Tawny-orange wings
aflutter, monarchs zigzag,
soar, drum milkweed buds.

In flight, all's wondrous dreaming.
On earth, turtle harvest. Lost.

Parched pink petunias
eight days in an empty house.
Gray cat grows lonely.

While tanned girls sway their wet braids
splashing rivers of laughter.

Whitecaps swirl, frolic
on Chesapeake Bay's sandy
shores — midsummer pearls.

Seaside, the nostalgic crab
dreams of walking back in time.

Robins remember
spring grasses — now scorched, blanched, crunched.
Hard earth resists beaks.

Yet from the old wistful tree
plums fall into tiny hands.

Sonorous ode — these
deciduous limbs tossing
their indulgent fruit.

Terra Mater purged, plundered,
trembles and weeps, but lives on.

Touched by the bee's kiss —
amor, amour, amore.
Fertility seized.

Orange blossoms all afire
plan weddings with grasshoppers.

Black-eyed Susans, wild
and willowy, flirt with wasps
mating in full sun.

Big Dipper starred in *Night's Sky*,
Megrez, its leading lady.

Courtesan to all,
your silvery fingers grip,
pull us to Heaven.

Paradise quite imperfect,
for love's left behind on Earth.

What have we humans
done? Tremors shake, roil coastlands.
Irene roars ashore.

Temblors cease once peace is made
with Mother, feverish, mad.

Ozone opening,
magenta madness expands,
breeds daughter's distress.

Verses lay down on the roofs.
Hurricane kissed them good night.

Gale force storm silenced,
begonias sluggish in shade —
the catcall of sleep.

Fixed to us: dirt, dust, drama
of countless rainy seasons.

Aires de verano
(Summer Wind)

Translated by Flor Aguilera García

Un viento estival de camino al sur
vierte calor en la noche expectante.
La luna se desvanece en el amanecer.

Los días nadan por los ríos como carpas,
lentamente hacia mares oscuros.

De los cielos destello y parpadeo.
Las luciérnagas perforan el ébano,
pasajes de bruma resplandecen.

Lágrimas felices desde el reinado de Tláloc
acogen con beneplácito al tierno maíz.

Nubes que velan lunas de aguamiel.
Aquí las oraciones provienen de tierras planas.
Los Padres sollozan — los perros rastrean.

Tangaras, arriba en sus nidos
ruegan a la misericordiosa Serpiente Emplumada.

Barco de pesca abandonado,
un tornado o una revuelta,
¿A dónde se han ido todos sus fantasmas?

Se han convertido en céfiro y suave brisa —
dulces caricias tropicales.

Dos gansos con sus crías.
Fuertes lazos familiares
al crecer montarán el Euros.

Praderas negras de ondeada seda
en una lenta danza lunar.

Estrellas etéreas
caen sobre colinas de trigo reluciente:
un prisma de gemas.

El canto de ave de amanecer: juego pío,
silencio, la mañana llueve.

Fragmentos de luz de luna descienden
a través de cenizas — patrones cortados con verde.
Los lirios blancos tiemblan.

Festín de colibríes, un melancólico néctar.
El agave azul está en flor.

Alas de bermejo
aletean, las monarcas vuelan en zigzag,
se disparan, se nutren de algodoncillo.

En vuelo, todo es asombroso soñar.
En la tierra, cosecha de las tortugas perdida.

Petunias muertas en rosa
ocho días de una casa vacía.
El gato gris se siente solo.

Mientras que las chicas bronceadas columpian sus trenzas
    mojadas —
salpicando ríos de risas.

Crestas de olas, remolinos enfiestados
en la arenosa Bahía de Chesapeake
orillas, perlas a medio verano.

En la playa, el nostálgico cangrejo
sueña con marchar hacia atrás, en el tiempo.

Los petirrojos recuerdan
pastos de primavera — ahora quemados, blanqueados,
    aplastados.
La tierra dura, resistente a picos.

Sin embargo, desde el anciano y melancólico árbol
caen las ciruelas en manos diminutas.

Oda sonora — estas
extremidades de hojas caducas lanzando
su fruto indulgente.

Terra Mater purgada, saqueada,
tiembla y llora, pero sigue aquí.

Tocado por el beso de la abeja —
amor, amour, amore.
Fertilidad incautada.

El azahar, ardiente fuego,
planea su boda con un saltamontes.

Susanas de ojos negros, salvajes
y esbeltas, coquetean con las avispas
apareamiento a pleno sol.

A Mayor, el protagonista del Cielo de Noche,
tendrá la estrella Megrez de primera dama.

Cortesana de todos,
sus dedos argentados nos toman,
nos jalan hacia el cielo.

El paraíso es bastante imperfecto,
pues el amor se queda atrás en la Tierra.

¿Qué han hecho los seres
humanos? Hacer temblar, sacudir, enturbiar las costas.
Irene ruge en tierra.

Los temblores cesarán una vez que se logre hacer las paces
con la Madre, febril, enloquecida.

El ozono es la apertura,
la locura magenta se expande,
da a luz a la angustia de la hija.

Los versos se recuestan sobre los techos.
El huracán les dio su beso de buenas noches.

La fuerza de la tormenta silenciada,
las begonias aletargadas en la sombra —
el silbido del sueño.

Quedan impregnados en nosotros: la suciedad, el polvo,
    el teatro
de todas las estaciones de lluvia.

Autumn Rain

Joyce Brinkman, Kae Morii, Carolyn Kreiter-Foronda

Fall's moon does not shine.
Storm volleys hammer windows.
Missing light and you.

My loneliness passes through
the road filled with bush clovers.

I feel you in fog
lingering past nightfall's bell.
Hummingbird: *stay! stay!*

Stay! Merry light of houses
on silent water surface.

Water washes leaves
from the gray elm tree's branches.
Shadows stalk the moon.

I oar a small boat to slip
through golden ripples to sky.

Douse me in Heaven's
holy song. See how dawn's glow
pours from a wren's mouth?

A rose perfumes longing for
you, standing by the holly wreath.

Smoke's aroma coils
from chimneys chastened since spring.
The bell's *riin-riin* fades.

In the calendar of blooms
you come, calling my dear name.

At daybreak our vows
echo from steep canyon's walls.
Oh, the wind's huge heart!

Of the verdure, the forest
has air and play of sunlight.

Woodland deer frolic.
Come! Tonight we ride moon's boat
through untainted seas.

Snail walks on a watery line.
Tearful eyes see welcome rain.

I extend my arms
and give you rainbow's gemmed light.
Wear it as jewels.

In open palms of green child,
one small granite stone holds God.

The red plum's stone waits.
Watch! Dwell in expectation.
Iris will return.

Passengers have gone and come —
an umbrella left in phantasm.

Fly, umbrella bird.
Spread your wings. Protect us. Share
the world's ambrosial fruit.

Not a blast. The divine wind
weakens us, relays wisdom.

Ghostly glass rattles.
Panes tempered with peace hold firm.
Shingles overlap.

My poor youth, recall again.
Bright poplar tree in blue sky!

Wise old oak, tell me:
Where is the mythical horse
of my childhood dreams?

Worrisome evening sun sets.
Flute tones in melancholy.

Will freedom's drum strokes
reverberate lovingly?
My mother's voice chants.

The future knows us. With hope,
any road reaches to rich land.

Embrace a handful
of my motherland's roan soil.
Know the farmer's joy!

Crossing the scarlet horizon,
tomorrow comes. Oh my darkness!

Can the moonlight dry
red tears from burning bushes?
Cry, cry for morning!

Joblessness deepens grass dews.
What's the essence in this world?

I whisper the word
calm like a mantra — and there
blooms raspberry day.

Colorful vision becomes vain.
The rose sea, spread at dawn.

River birch drinks deep,
yet tan bark splits into curls.
Cruel cuts at dusk!

Breeze blows, time steals, and we find
clear moon on thin ice calms me.

Icicle pansies
and violas lift their heads —
Bless Thanksgiving's sun.

Winter will pierce black earth. O!
Magnolia buds — soon spring's crown.

秋雨
(Autumn Rain)

Translated by Kae Morii

窓を打つ雨に君想う月も見えず

侘しくも一人ゆく萩の道

夕暮れの鐘の音ひびき止まれハチドリ

留めよ　水面の家の明かりを

濯がれし楡の枝月に忍び寄る

天のさざ波櫂でこぎゆく

聖らかな夜明けを歌うミソサザイ

薔薇の花かおり柊を恋い慕う

霞ゆく煙突のけむりベルの音

花暦たずねて歩く君の名を

峡谷に声響き吹く風わたる

新緑の森に射す木漏れ日

朗らかな鹿を誘う月の小舟

なみだ道歩む蝸牛に雨

虹の空ひかりの宝石きみに贈る

みどり児の手に神在す小石

心ありてあやめふり向く梅の実かな

過ぎ行く者の忘れ傘ひとつ

飛べカサドリ　世界の果実わかちあい

天啓の風　叡智つたえよ

がたがたと揺れる窓ガラス映る屋根

子ども時代のポプラと青空

樫の木よ　告げよ神話の馬の行方

笛の音悲しく夕日愁える

鳴り響け自由のドラム母の声

未来は希望とともに豊かさへ

一握の土に交じり合う喜びあり

夕焼け空の明日と暗闇

燃える藪泣きはらす眼に月の光

この世の糧を露草に問う

真言の祈りにそよぐ果実の日々

空しさが色づく曙光の海よ

闇に悲し　たゆたう川の秋の色

忍びよる風に薄氷の月

凍えても手をかざす花に日は微笑み

悲しみに夢みる　木蓮の花冠

Winter Sky

Joyce Brinkman, Gabriele Glang, Carolyn Kreiter-Foronda

December sky spits.
Shooting stars speed over earth.
Words traverse the sea.

A snow-globe blizzard swirls — ah! —
syllables settle: two lines.

Up they whirl — eddies
of flakes lit up like fireflies:
Christmas on the Bay.

Epiphany's constellations
portend a coming sea change.

Three strangers appear.
Shadows in missing moonlight.
Winter rabbits feed.

Crows converge invisibly,
maudlin above bare larch woods.

A tremulous wail:
an owl's screech burrows through night —
those golden eyes masked.

My thorny longings scuffle —
panic in the underbrush!

Devotion holds strong.
Red-tailed hawk chooses his feast.
Doves separated.

Raptor's aching hunger reigns:
ah! — love's trail of breadcrumbs ends —

A buoyant swoosh! Two
bald eagles stir dawn's shrill glow:
river guardians.

Icy shards clog brittle shores,
water's muddy meander.

Even sun's rays fail.
Contentment escapes cold bones.
Dreams of Half-Moon Bay.

Above pale, frost-hard acres
the bitten-down wafer wanes.

Billowing: green wings
of hollies, their berries gone.
Cleanse me, winter winds.

A brambly sloe hedge shelters
the greenfinch clan's reunion.

Sparrows search for warmth —
discover heated birdbath.
Chrysanthemum tea.

In my cup milk blooms — one tear
disturbs this chill, murky pond.

Ice floes wash ashore
in twilight's rose overture —
evening's indulgence.

Tangerine orb swells, leaking
into pines. Snowfields glimmer.

Harrier circles.
Sapor of death in stale air.
Shots! Officer down.

Silence floods morning's wreckage.
Grey heron stands sentinel.

Camellias recoil.
In Egypt, uprisings mount.
A lagoon empties.

Puddles glint in neap's retreat:
cerulean sequins mudflats.

Cardinals share
morsels freed from servitude.
Retreat, bitter heart.

Chiffchaffs agitate in shrubs:
raucous din of pairing off.

Jonquils inch through soil.
Who can ignore wisps of spring
igniting the soul?

One last fling: carnivalesque
confetti shrouds crocus tips.

Moon drained of silver.
Monetary depletion.
World's nations bicker.

A magpie-ruckus erupts —
food fights among the coal tits.

At the feeders, red-
winged blackbirds spar with grackles.
Peace, the heavens plead.

But greed rules: poultry tussles
send feathers sailing earthward.

Squirrels bounce berries
from frozen trees. Snow storms stalk
Ides of March Madness.

Dervish gusts empty beeches —
send leaf tatters scurrying.

I pluck African
violet blues from my mind —
freedom on the rise.

High above dun fields larks sing —
at last! — I hear sap rising.

Winterhimmel
(Winter Sky)

Translated by Gabriele Glang

Dezemberhimmel spuckt.
Sternschnuppen eilen über Erde.
Worte kreuzen Meer.

Schneekugelsturm wirbelt — ah! —
Silben legen sich: zwei Zeilen.

Flockenwirbel strudeln
aufwärts — ein Glühwurmleuchten:
Die Bucht weihnachtet.

Rauhnächtliche Sternenbilder
verkünden Veränderung.

Drei Fremde tauchen auf.
Schatten in vermisstem Mondschein.
Winterhasen fressen.

Unsichtbar versammeln sich Krähen,
klagend über nackten Lärchen.

Furchtsames Klagen:
Eulenschrei durchbohrt die Nacht —
Goldaugen maskiert.

Mein stacheliges Sehnen
im Zwist — Panik im Gestrüpp!

Hingabe verbindet.
Rotschwanzbussard wählt sein Festmahl.
Tauben, getrennt.

Greifvogels Hunger herrscht: ah! —
Brotkrumenliebesspur reißt ab —

Schwungvolles Sausen! Zwei
Adler schüren schrille Morgenglut —
Wächter des Flusses.

Eisscherben am spröden Ufer
hemmen trübes Mäandern.

Selbst Sonnenstrahlen schlagen fehl.
Kalten Knochen entwischt Heiterkeit.
Half-Moon Bay Träume.

Über frostbleichen Ackern
schwindet die angenagte Hostie.

Grün wogend: Flügel
der Stechpalmen, beerenlos.
Heile mich, Winterwind.

Dornige Schlehen schützen
Grünfink-Clans Wiedersehen.

Spatzen suchen Wärme,
entdecken beheiztes Vogelbad.
Chrysanthementee.

Milch blüht in meiner Tasse —
eine Träne trübt den kalten Teich.

Eisschollen schwemmen Ufersaum
im rosa Dämmerungsauftakt —
des Abends Genuss.

Himmelsfrucht schwillt an, ein Leck
in Kiefern. Schneefelder glimmen.

Die Feldweihe kreist.
Todesgeruch in schaler Luft.
Schüsse! Offizier getroffen.

Stille umspült Morgentrümmer.
Ein Graureiher steht Wache.

Kamelien entziehen sich.
In Ägypten wächst Aufstand.
Eine Lagune versickert.

Nipptide besetzt das Watt
mit Pailletten, himmelblau.

Kardinäle teilen
von Knechtschaft befreite Happen.
Zurück, bittres Herz.

Im Gebüsch eifern Zilpzalps:
lärmender Paarungskrakeel.

Narzissenstreben.
Wer kann den seelenzündenen
Frühjahrshauch übersehen?

Ein letzter Wurf: Karnevals-
konfetti bedeckt Krokusse.

Mond seines Silbers
entleert. Monetärer Schwund.
Weltnationen streiten.

Ein Elsterkrawall bricht aus —
Tannenmeisen Futterschlacht.

Vogelhausgerangel
unter Rotschulterstärlingen.
Frieden, fleht der Himmel.

Doch Gier regiert. Federvieh
rauft sich — erdwärts schweben Daunen.

Eichhörnchen schicken Beeren
von vereisten Bäumen. Schneestürme
lauern — März Wahnsinn.

Dervisch Bö fegt Buchen leer —
Blattfetzen hasten davon.

Ich pflücke Usambara-
veilchen-*Blues* aus meinem Kopf —
Freiheit im Aufbruch.

Hoch über braunen Feldern: Lerchenlied.
Endlich! hör ich Säfte steigen.

The Poets

Flor Aguilera García

Flor Aguilera García is a poet and fiction writer. Her poetry books include *Last Flight to Shanghai* (Praxis, 2002), *The Sacrifice of the Lilies* (Praxis, 2003), *55 Frames Per Second* (Praxis, 2005), *BUTOH* (Tintanueva, 2008) and *As the Audience Begs for a Ferocious Tango* (San Francisco Bay Press, 2010). She has also written several novels, among them: *Diary of an Oyster* (Alfaguara, 2005), *My Life as a Blonde* (Alfaguara, 2008), and *The Past is a Strange Country* (Suma, 2013). She also recently published her first book of short stories for children, *The Day Grandmother Exploded* (Alfaguara, 2013). She has participated in several international poetry festivals: Trois Rivières, Cartagena,

Bucharest, and as international guest in the Poets Laureate of America gathering in Indianapolis in 2007. She lives in Mexico City in the nostalgic Roman Quarter.

Flor Aguilera García es poeta y narradora. Entre sus libros de poesía se encuentran: *El último vuelo a Shanghai* (Praxis, 2002), *El sacrificio de los lirios* (Praxis, 2003), *55 cuadros por segundo* (Praxis, 2005), *Butoh* (Tinta nueva, 2008) y *As the Audience Begs for a Ferocious Tango* (San Francisco Bay Press, 2010). También ha escrito varias novelas, entre ellos: *Diario de un Oyster* (Alfaguara, 2005), *Mi vida como una rubia* (Alfaguara, 2008), *El pasado es un país extraño* (Suma, 2013). Este año publicó su primer libro de cuentos para niños, *El día que explotó la abuela* (Alfaguara, 2013). Ha participado en diversos Festivales Internacionales de Poesía: Trois Rivières, Cartagena, Bucarest y como invitada internacional en la reunión de los Poetas Laureados de Estados Unidos, que se llevó a cabo en Indianápolis en 2007. Vive en la Ciudad de México, en la nostálgica Colonia Roma.

Catherine Aubelle

Catherine Aubelle is a self-taught artist and writer of fiction and poetry. As a girl, her first mentor was a fatherly architect, who took her under his wing and taught her about making art and poetry. Her first drama, *Titus*, was performed when she was a teenager at Maison de la Culture d'Amiens (1979), and she published fiction and poetry in the local newspapers. She moved to London in 1981, where she worked for several years as an illustrator for print media and television, acquiring skills in the field of animation, as well. After her return to Paris in 1985, she continued to work as an illustrator and writer for the French weeklies and children's book publishers. She subsequently spent several years traveling and working in Africa, where she continued to hone her writing and art, drawing on the experience of living in the bush. In 1992 Les Editions du Seuil published her first children's book, *Capucine est partie*. Like her visual work, her writing crosses genres and can best be classified as short poetic stories.

She has taught creative writing to all age groups and levels in schools, libraries, associations, adult education, jails, and psychiatric hospitals. In some cases, this work has resulted in published anthologies, which she managed and edited, e.g., *Prises de mots, L'Enfer me ment* (Harmattan). She has been awarded several artists' residencies, notably Biblithèque de Nevers and Salon du Livre de Bordeaux. In recent years, she has devoted time to a wide variety of projects both as writer and painter. In 2011, her children's book *Capucine est partie* was adapted for the dance theater by Le Safran in Amiens. She is currently involved in an international joint artistic and literary venture with German-American artist and writer Gabriele Glang. They published a trilingual poetry collection in 2012 called *Dialogues*. In 2013, they published a trilingual works catalogue, *Palimpsests*, which also features their haikus and tankas.

Catherine Aubelle est une artiste autodidacte et écrivaine de fiction et de poésie. Enfant, son premier mentor était un architecte, qui l'a prise sous son aile et lui inculqua quelques rudiments à propos de l'art et de la poésie. Sa première pièce, *Titus*, fut jouée lorsqu'elle était adolescente à la Maison de la Culture d'Amiens (1979), alors qu'elle publiait ses histoires et ses poèmes dans les journaux locaux. Elle s'installa à Londres en 1981, où elle travailla plusieurs années en tant qu'illustratrice pour la presse et la télévision, acquérant également des compétences dans le domaine de l'animation. Lors de son retour à Paris en 1985, elle continua de travailler en tant qu'illustratrice et auteur pour les journaux hebdomadaires et éditeurs français. Elle passa ces années à voyager en Afrique, où elle continua de perfectionner son écriture et son art, dessinant d'après son expérience de la vie dans la brousse. En 1992, les Editions du Seuil publient son premier livre pour la jeunesse, *Capucine est partie*. Comme ses œuvres visuelles, son écriture traverse les genres et peut être classifiée dans celui des nouvelles poétiques. Ce livre a été adapté pour le ballet théâtre (Le Safran), à Amiens en 1994.

Elle a enseigné l'écriture créative pour des groupes de tout âge et niveau, dans les écoles, les bibliothèques, les associations, en milieu carcéral, et psychiatrique. A plusieurs reprises, ces travaux ont fait l'objet de publications (*Prises de mots, l'Enfer me ment* – Harmattan). Plusieurs résidences d'artistes lui ont été accordées (Bibliothèque de Nevers, Salon du Livre de Bordeaux). Ces dernières années, elle a consacré son temps à des activités plus larges en tant qu'écrivain et peintre. Elle est actuellement engagée dans une entreprise artistique et littéraire internationale avec l'artiste et écrivaine germano-américaine Gabriele Glang. Elles ont publié un recueil trilingue de poésie, *Dialogues* en 2012. En 2013, elles ont publié un catalogue trilingue de leurs travaux, *Palimpsestes*, qui présente également leurs haïkus et tankas.

www.aubelleglangencounters.com

Joyce Brinkman

Joyce Brinkman served as Indiana's first poet laureate from 2002–2008. She has a BA from Hanover College, Indiana. She began writing poetry at age nine and was first published in *Hill Thoughts*. Her book, *Tiempo Español,* was written in Spain, where she studied with the University of New Orleans MFA program. Her poetry has appeared in newspapers, magazines, and on CDs, postcards, bookmarks and buses, as well as on a wall in the town square of Quezaltepeque, El Salvador.

Joyce is one of six poets whose poetry is represented in 25-foot, stained glass windows at the Indianapolis International Airport. A group of those poets have produced a book of travel metaphor, *Rivers, Rails and Runways,* and a book of postcard poems, *Airmail from the Airpoets.* She also collaborated with glass artist Arlon Bayliss on lighted glass art containing her poetry for the new addition of the Marion County Central Library. She is a strong proponent of poetry as public art and enjoys working with both visual and literary artists on projects.

Joyce helped start the Indiana Poetry Out Loud Program and has often served as a judge for the state finals. She is a founding board member of Brick Street Poetry Inc., which is the sponsoring organization for the award-winning project, Word Hunger, and in 2012 organized Indy Literary Arts, a new group to promote the literary arts in Central Indiana. Joyce has read at libraries, universities, and other venues across the country. She counts the Poetry at Noon, 2008, Library of Congress program with her fellow Airpoets as her favorite reading.

She has received residency fellowships from Mary Anderson Center for the Arts and the Vermont Studio. She used a two-year Creative Renewal Fellowship from the Arts Council of Indianapolis to connect the inspiration she received from her time in Spain with the Central American Hispanic culture through the teaching of soccer/poetry clinics in El Salvador. In 2013, she received an Indiana Individual Artist grant to explore cross-species poetic collaborations with orang-utans at the new International Orangutan Center at the Indianapolis Zoo.

Joyce shares a house in Indianapolis, IN, with her husband and a sweet cat named Bobb. She and Bobb contemplate the world of nature as they spy on wildlife at the pond just beyond their backyard. She also seeks solitude for writing at a condo in West Palm Beach, FL.

Gabriele Glang

Born and raised in the USA, German-American **Gabriele Glang** has been writing and painting all her life, publishing her first poems at age 16. She received her BA in English Writing from George Mason University in Fairfax, VA. After completing a graduate publications specialist program at George Washington University, Washington, DC, she self-published *Roundelay*, a chapbook of poems. She was a fellow of the Virginia Center of the Creative Arts in 1988. She spent many years working in the publishing business as an editor and graphic artist in the nation's capital before relocating to the country of her ancestors, southern Germany, in 1990. That year, SCOP Publications published her volume of poetry, *Stark Naked on a Cold Irish Morning.*

She now lives with her family in a tiny rural village on the Swabian Alp in Baden-Württemberg. Here she works as a freelance teacher, translator, writer, and painter. A bilingual poet, she has published poetry in the US and Europe, and in 2004 she received a stipend from the Society for the Advancement of Writers in Baden-Württemberg for her German poetry. In addition, she writes screenplays for television and cinema. In 2008 she received script development funding from the Media and Film Board Baden-Württemberg for a screenplay about the German Expressionist painter, Paula Modersohn-Becker. Gabriele Glang is associate professor of creative writing at the University of Esslingen, and teaches writing and painting workshops in private industry, adult education, and private workshops to all age groups and for all levels. She has been an artist/writer-in-residence in Soltau, Germany, three times and was a resident in the Brecht House in Svendborg, Denmark. A landscape painter, she has exhibited her pastels in the US, Germany, France, and Poland. She is currently involved in an international joint artistic and literary venture with French painter and writer Catherine Aubelle. They published a trilingual poetry collection in 2012 called *Dialogues.* In fall 2013 they published a trilingual works catalogue, *Palimpsests,* which features their haikus and tankas.

Geboren und aufgewachsen in den USA, schreibt und malt die zweisprachige Deutsch-Amerikanerin **Gabriele Glang** seit jeher. Ihre ersten Gedichte veröffentlichte sie mit 16 Jahren. Ihren Bachelor of Arts in Anglistik machte sie an der George Mason University in Fairfax, VA. Nach einem Publizistik Studiengang an der George Washington University in Washington, DC, veröffentlichte sie einen Lyrikband im Eigenverlag, *Roundelay*. Im Jahr 1988 erhielt sie ein Stipendium im Virginia Center for the Creative Arts. She arbeitete viele Jahre als Lektorin und Grafikerin im Verlagssektor in Washington, DC, bevor sie 1990 in die Heimat ihrer Vorfahren umsiedelte. Im selben Jahr veröffentlichte SCOP Publications ihre Lyrik, *Stark Naked on a Cold Irish Morning*.

Sie lebt mit ihrer Familie in einem kleinen Dorf auf der Schwäbischen Alb. Hier unterrichtet, übersetzt, schreibt und malt die Freiberuflerin. Des Weiteren veröffentlicht die zweisprachige Lyrikerin mittlerweile nicht nur deutsche Lyrik, für die sie 2004 ein Stipendium vom Förderkreis deutscher Schriftsteller Baden-Württemberg erhielt, sondern schreibt Drehbücher in englischer und deutscher Sprache. Im Jahr 2008 erhielt sie eine Drehbuchförderung von der Medien und Filmgesellschaft Baden-Württemberg für einen Kinospielfilm über die deutsche Expressionistin Paula Modersohn-Becker. Gabriele Glang ist Dozentin für kreatives Schreiben und Englisch an der Hochschule Esslingen, sie unterrichtet zudem Schreiben und Malerei in der Industrie, in der Erwachsenenbildung, sowie privat für alle Altersgruppen und Stufen. Sie ist mehrfach als Stadtschreiberin und Künstlerin in der Soltauer Künstlerwohnung zu Gast gewesen, sowie im Brecht Haus in Svendborg, Dänemark. Als Landschaftsmalerin stellt sie ihre Pastellbilder in den USA, Deutschland, Frankreich und Polen aus. Zusammen mit der französischen Malerin und Autorin Catherine Aubelle ist sie derzeit mit einem internationalen Gemeinschaftsprojekt unterwegs. Sie haben im vergangenen Jahr eine dreisprachige Lyriksammlung unter dem Titel *Dialoge* veröffentlicht. Im Herbst 2013 veröffentlichten sie einen dreisprachigen Werkkatalog, in dem auch ihre Haikus und Tankas erschienen.

www.gabrieleglang.de
www.aubelleglangencouters.com

Carolyn Kreiter-Foronda

Carolyn Kreiter-Foronda served as Poet Laureate of the Commonwealth of Virginia from 2006–2008. She holds a BA from the University of Mary Washington and a MEd, MA and a PhD from George Mason University, where she received the institution's first doctorate, as well as a Scholarship and Service Award and a Letter of Recognition for Quality Research from the Virginia Educational Research Association for her dissertation, *Gathering Light: A Poet's Approach to Poetry Analysis.* In 2007 both universities gave her the Distinguished Alumna of the Year Award. In 2008 she was inducted into Phi Beta Kappa (Kappa of Virginia) at the University of Mary Washington.

She has published six books of poetry: *Contrary Visions, Gathering Light, Death Comes Riding, Greatest Hits, River Country,* and *The Embrace: Diego Rivera and Frida Kahlo.* She has also co-edited *In a Certain Place,* an anthology, and *Four Virginia Poets Laureate: A Teaching Guide.* Her poems have been nominated for six Pushcart Prizes and appear widely in publications, such as *Nimrod, Prairie Schooner, Mid-American Review, Hispanic Culture Review, Best of Literary Journals, Anthology of Magazine Verse & Yearbook of American Poetry, Poet Lore,* and *An Endless Skyway,* an anthology of poems by US State Poets Laureate.

Her numerous awards include five grants from the Virginia Commission for the Arts; a *Spree* First Place award; multiple awards in Pen Women competitions; a Special Merit Poem in *Comstock Review's* Muriel Craft Bailey Memorial contest; a *Passages North* contest award; an Edgar Allan Poe first-place award; a Virginia Cultural Laureate Award; and a Resolution of Appreciation from the State Board of Education for her contributions as Poet Laureate of Virginia. She has taught grades K–12, college/university courses, and poetry workshops in nursing homes, art galleries, and homeless shelters. Her many teaching awards include a National Scholastic Teaching Portfolio Award, a Rotary Meritorious Educator of the Year Award, and a Hodgson Award for Excellence in Teaching English.

She currently serves as a Literary Arts Specialist on a Metrorail Public Art Project, which will integrate poems, including her own, into art installations at metro stations in Northern Virginia. Carolyn is an accomplished visual artist, whose works have been widely displayed. She teaches art-inspired poetry workshops for the Virginia Museum of Fine Arts.

www.carolynforonda.com
http://en.wikipedia.org/wiki/Carolyn_Kreiter-Foronda

Kae Morii

Kae Morii is a Japanese poet who is active in the international poetry world. She was born in Osaka, Japan, and graduated from Keio University with a BA. Her first book, *A Red Currant,* was published in 1997, followed by *Homage to the Light,* a poetry and art collection. In 2003, she published *The light of lapis lazuli,* a collaboration with famous Japanese artist Kojin Kudo (member of the World Academy of Art and Culture). After her first English poem was used in the prevention campaign against terror, she published English poems in *World Congress of Poets* and her poetry was introduced in many magazines, newspapers, and anthologies around the world. In 2007, she was invited to the US by Indiana Poet Laureate Joyce Brinkman for the 3rd Annual Gathering of State Poets Laureate, where she shared her poetry on the CD *Sporting Words*. That poetic meeting opened her eyes to the world even more. Subsequently, she published the English version of *Over the Endless Night* in Japan; then *Cabbage Field & Wind Power Generators* in Romania, by Dr. Dumitru Ion in 2008; *Mega Quake, Tsunami, and Fukushima;* and *Olive — A Letter from Anne Frank* in 2012. She has been invited to many international poetry festivals and gatherings for peace. Her poems have received numerous awards and literature prizes. Since 2010, she has served as the first examiner of the UNESCO youth poetry contests in Japan.

森井香衣、日本の国際派詩人。大阪生まれ、慶應義塾大学卒。第一詩集は、1997年、『すぐりの樹』。2003年『光のオマージュ』、日本画画伯工藤甲人氏との詩画集『瑠璃光』。初めて書いた英詩がテロ防止キャンペーンで使われてから、世界詩人大会などで英詩を発表し、広く海外の新聞、雑誌、アンソロジーに紹介される。2006年モンゴルのメンド・オーヨー氏訳『風とわたし』。2007年、インディアナ州桂冠詩人ジョイス・ブリンクマン会長から、第3回米国桂冠詩人年次大会に 招待され、CD『スポーツのことば』に参加。その詩的な出 会いは、彼女の目を世界に向け、2008年、英詩集『果てしない夜へ』、ルーマニアのドミトル・

イオン氏訳による 『キャベツ畑と風力発電機』、
2012年、『66-巨大地 震、津波、そして福島』、
『オリーブ-アンネからの 手紙』を発表。彼女は、
広く国際詩祭に参加し、平和に貢献している。
文学賞など数々受賞。2010年か
らユネスコポエム大賞の審査委員長を務める。

About the Type

This book was set in ITC Galliard®, a contemporary adaptation of Robert Granjon's 16th century typeface design by Matthew Carter. The ITC Galliard® font captures the vitality of Granjon's work in a graceful, modern typeface. The Japanese font is MS Mincho® by Microsoft.

Designed by John Taylor-Convery
Composed at JTC Imagineering, Santa Maria,CA